CIVIL RIGHTS STORIES

Human Rights

Written by Louise Spilsbury with illustrations by Toby Newsome

FRANKLIN WATTS
LONDON · SYDNEY

Foreword by Professor Leslie Thomas QC

Having spent a career fighting for civil rights, this book was a welcome delight to read. Enforcement and protection of our human rights are essential for a fair, free and democratic society. We often hear that someone's human rights have been breached. However, now we have a book for younger readers explaining why this might be so.

To take human rights seriously we need to properly educate ourselves and our children with what these words really mean. For when we all stand up together for human rights this is an extremely powerful thing to behold. The global Black Lives Matter protests are testament to that fact.

I wish when I was younger I had a book that explained in clear terms what human rights are. Where they come from. Why they are important and why we should never be complacent about them. This book does exactly that. No progressive children's library is complete without this book.

Professor Leslie Thomas QC, LLB (Hons); LLD (*honoris causa*)
Human Rights and Civil Liberties Barrister of Garden Court Chambers

Professor Leslie Thomas QC, has been described as a 'voice for the dead'. For more than 25 years Leslie has appeared in some of the highest profile inquests in the country. In 2012 he was awarded Legal Aid Barrister of the Year LALY. Louise Christian of Christian Khan solicitors stated "Leslie has done more for the families of those who die in custody or at the hands of the police than any other single lawyer. This is extremely difficult and not well funded work which requires extraordinary dedication and persistence and Leslie has all these things as well as enormous empathy with clients." In 2013 Kingston University awarded him an Honorary Doctorate for services for civil rights. In 2014 he was awarded Queen's Counsel. In 2016 he received a second LALY award for his work on Hillsborough. In 2017 he became Joint Head of Garden Court Chambers. In 2017 he was also awarded the Lifetime Achievement Award in the UK Diversity Legal Awards from BSN. Leslie is featured in the cinema documentary *Injustice* (2001) and *Who Polices the Police* (2012) by Ken Fero and was legal advisor on the BBC drama *Undercover*. In 2020 Leslie was appointed Professor of Law at Gresham College. The Law Professorship at Gresham College is over four centuries old and has been held by some of the nation's leading lawyers and legal academics.

CONTENTS

What are human rights?	4
Human rights in the past	6
Rights and revolution	8
After the Second World War	10
Fighting for women's rights	12
Children's rights	14
The right to speak our minds	16
Education for all	18
The right to water	20
Freedom from violence	22
Freedom from slavery	24
The right to a healthy world	26
Human rights today	28
Human rights timeline	30
Glossary and books to read	31
Index	32

WHAT ARE HUMAN RIGHTS?

A right is something a person is allowed to do, to have, or to be that should never be taken away from them. Human rights are the rights we all have from the day we are born. Our human rights are very important and they affect all our lives, every day.

Among the most basic human rights are the right to live, to have food and somewhere safe to live. Other human rights include the right to freedom, to travel, to be treated fairly and equally, to live safely and in peace, and to go to school.

We often take our human rights for granted, but human rights protect us and help us to get along with each other and live in peace. What would life be like if these rights were taken away?

Nobody has to earn their human rights. These rights apply to all humans, everywhere.

HUMAN RIGHTS IN THE PAST

Throughout most of human history, people did not have rights. How safe and free someone was depended in part on luck and in part on which family or group they belonged to.

The ancient Greeks were among the first people to talk about human rights. They believed in what they called natural law. Natural law is the idea that there are rules people follow because they are simply the right things to do, unlike laws that leaders make up or people agree on. They said that natural law gave certain rights to everyone, everywhere.

The first time people wrote a whole document about human rights was 1215. The Magna Carta, which means 'great charter', set out the rights of the people of England and stated that the law applies to everyone. It was written to stop the king breaking laws and treating his people unfairly. It was signed by King John on 12 June 1215.

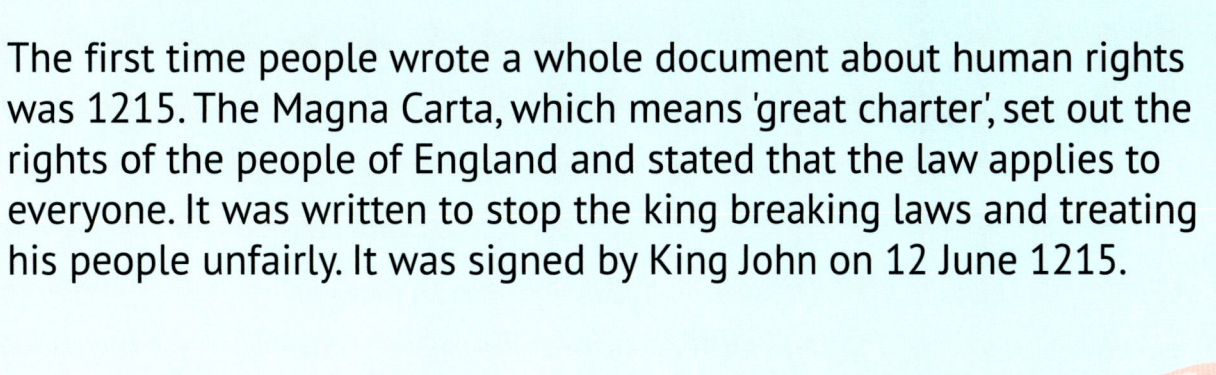

The Magna Carta was an important document that inspired the fight for human rights in other countries.

RIGHTS AND REVOLUTION

Change was slow to come, so by the 18th century some people led revolutions to win their rights. In America, people fought violent battles to break free of British rule and become independent. In 1776, in their Declaration of Independence, the leaders of the new United States of America listed "Life, Liberty, and the pursuit of Happiness" as rights due to all men.

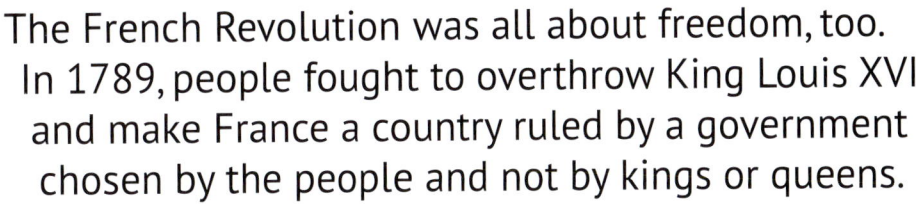

King Louis XVI

The French Revolution was all about freedom, too. In 1789, people fought to overthrow King Louis XVI and make France a country ruled by a government chosen by the people and not by kings or queens.

When the people succeeded, the French government also wrote a declaration setting out people's new rights. These included the freedom to follow the religion you choose and the freedom to say what you believe.

These declarations sounded good, but they didn't help everyone. In the USA, for example, rights were denied to women, Black people, Native Americans and people without property.

By the 20th century, people were starting to change this inequality, but then two world wars happened and people were too busy trying to survive to fight for their rights.

AFTER THE SECOND WORLD WAR

Millions of people were killed and millions more were forced from their homes in both the First World War (1914-18) and the Second World War (1939-45). The horrors of war finally shocked people into making a bigger effort to ensure everyone had the human rights they deserved.

In 1945, world leaders got together and set up a new organisation: the United Nations. The UN's aim was to prevent war and to build a better world.

Eleanor Roosevelt was a politician and an activist who was married to Franklin D. Roosevelt, President of the United States from 1933-45.

In 1945, Eleanor became the first chairperson of the UN to work for human rights. She played a big part in creating a list of the human rights that belong to everyone. It is called the Universal Declaration of Human Rights.

The Universal Declaration of Human Rights was signed in 1948 by many of the world's leaders. The leaders and their governments made a solemn promise to ensure everyone was given their rights.

FIGHTING FOR WOMEN'S RIGHTS

The human rights declarations were a fantastic achievement, but the problem is ensuring human rights really are enjoyed by all. Even when human rights are written into a country's law, some people still break these laws.

All over the world, the rights of women and girls are often ignored. Many ordinary people have banded together to fight to protect human rights.

For example, in many countries it is against the law to force a girl or woman to marry someone against her will. However, some girls are still made to marry much older men who they may have never met before. Many of these girls will be mistreated by their husbands.

Amnesty International is a group that investigates cases where human rights are ignored and helps people to claim their rights. For example, in Sierra Leone they teach young women about the dangers of early and forced marriage and train local adults to spot and report forced marriages to the police.

Knowing their rights and how to get help has saved many girls from a fate that robs them of childhood, puts them at risk of violence and even of death from having babies too young.

CHILDREN'S RIGHTS

In the past, many children around the world were expected to work. In some places, children as young as four years old were forced to do jobs. Many of these jobs, such as working in coal mines, put children in danger.

People began to realise that children needed some extra protections that adults don't. One example of this is in the world of work.

In 1959, the UN agreed a list of children's rights: the Declaration of the Rights of the Child. Countries signing the declaration promised to protect a long list of children's rights.

In 1989, an updated list called the United Nations Convention on the Rights of the Child was created. The list includes a child's right to live with their parents (unless it is unsafe at home), to play and go to school.

Governments also agree to set a minimum age for children to work and protect children from work that might stop them learning, playing and growing in safety.

Yet today, some child workers still illegally dig mines and labour on farms. They work machines in factories, become slaves in homes or even sell drugs on the streets.

THE RIGHT TO SPEAK OUR MINDS

Everyone's voice matters. We all have the right to think what we like, to say what we think and to share our ideas with other people. Unfortunately, there are governments and other powerful people around the world who find ways to restrict this key human right.

In some places, people who disagree with those in power and express those opinions in peaceful protests get into trouble. Some governments imprison, torture or even murder people for speaking out. Such governments may also stop newspapers and TV stations from criticising their decisions.

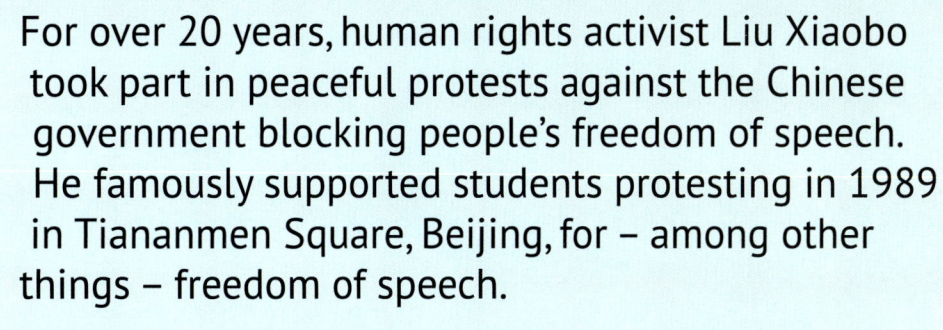
Liu Xiaobo

For over 20 years, human rights activist Liu Xiaobo took part in peaceful protests against the Chinese government blocking people's freedom of speech. He famously supported students protesting in 1989 in Tiananmen Square, Beijing, for – among other things – freedom of speech.

Xiaobo was arrested in December 2008, and sentenced to 11 years in prison for criticising the government. He was awarded the Nobel Peace Prize in 2010, while he was in jail, for his struggle for basic human rights in China. He inspired many others to do the same.

EDUCATION FOR ALL

Children's right to an education is essential because schooling affects our whole lives. School gives us the skills we need to get jobs and stay healthy. It teaches us about the world and our rights.

So, why don't millions of children get the education they deserve? Some girls are kept away from school because people don't think they need an education. Other families can't afford to pay for the books, uniforms, or transport their children need to go to school. In war zones, bombs may destroy school buildings or force people to flee, leaving their schools behind.

In 2008, Malala Yousafzai began to protest against the closing of girls' schools in the area of Pakistan where she lived. In 2012, she was shot while riding on her school bus in an attempt to silence her.

But Yousafzai survived. The attack made her famous and she used her fame to speak out about the importance of education for girls all over the world. In 2014, Malala won the Nobel Peace Prize.

Malala Yousafzai

THE RIGHT TO WATER

We all need water to survive. We need water for drinking and cooking, washing and cleaning, and for toilets that deal safely with human waste. That's why having water and sanitation are recognised as basic human rights.

A lack of clean water and sanitation causes hardship and suffering. People get sick or die from diseases spread by polluted or germ-filled water or a lack of sinks and toilets. People go hungry when farmers do not have enough water for crops and farm animals. If a well or water supply is far from a village, women and children spend hours collecting water instead of working, caring for their families or going to school.

Lead can pollute drinking water when pipes containing lead wear away. Lead-polluted water can make people very sick.

Gitanjali Rao, a young scientist from Colorado, USA, invented a cheap device that can quickly test water for pollutants like lead. She named it after Tethys, the Greek goddess of clean water. The invention won her the America's Top Young Scientist award in October 2017.

FREEDOM FROM VIOLENCE

We all have the right to live in freedom and safety. Sadly, many people around the world live in fear with the threat of violence hanging over them every day.

Some people are tortured in violent ways by governments who want to stop them speaking their minds. In wars, innocent people may be killed or an army may try to kill all of the people who belong to one particular group. In some places, children are forced to serve as soldiers in wars and lose their right to grow up in safety.

When Divina Maloum learned about children who were being forced to carry out bomb attacks, she took action. Aged just 15, she set up a group of young people to teach children in Cameroon to say no to violence.

Her organisation, Children for Peace, uses cartoons to explain the real horrors of terrorism and war. In 2019, Maloum was joint winner of the International Children's Peace Prize for her efforts.

Divina Maloum

FREEDOM FROM SLAVERY

Another very important human right is the right not to be a slave. A slave is owned by someone as if they are a piece of property. Slaves are forced to work for someone against their will. Slavery is illegal worldwide, yet many people are forced into slavery.

Around the world, many adults and children are tricked or violently taken from home and forced to live and work in a new place. This is called human trafficking. People trapped in this way are made to work in homes, farms, factories or on the streets. They are given little or no pay and rarely have time off. They are often cruelly treated, beaten and starved.

Anti-Slavery International is an organisation that tries to stop people being treated like slaves or made to work against their will. It encourages governments to make stronger laws. It helps adults and children to gain and keep their freedom. It builds schools for children who have escaped slavery and lends adults money to help them rebuild their lives in freedom.

THE RIGHT TO A HEALTHY WORLD

Clean water is just one part of the natural world we rely on for a healthy life. That's why more and more countries are agreeing that a healthy environment is a vital human right.

One of the biggest threats to the natural world is climate change. Human activities, such as burning fossil fuels to power vehicles, add gases to the atmosphere that trap heat and increase Earth's temperatures.

Warmer climates melt ice at the Poles, causing sea levels to rise and submerge low-lying coastlines and islands. Warmer ocean water harms marine wildlife and long, dry periods on land kill the farm crops we need to eat.

Climate change also increases the chances of deadly events such as ferocious wildfires, hurricane-force winds and heavy floods.

Many people and organisations are taking action on climate change, such as using solar or wind power instead of fossil fuels.

One of the most famous climate activists is the Swedish teenager Greta Thunberg. She has inspired millions of people to fight climate change and to join protests around the world. In September 2019, she gave a historic speech at a UN climate conference in New York, USA.

HUMAN RIGHTS TODAY

People around the world work every day to make our planet a better, fairer and more just place. Their efforts have made a huge difference. Many people enjoy all of their human rights, but sadly in some places, these rights are still denied.

On 10 December 1948, the United Nations celebrated the first Human Rights Day. Since then, every year on that day people take time to appreciate the effect that human rights declarations have on their lives. Victories in the fight for human rights are celebrated and events take place across the world to remind people why human rights matter.

We can all make a difference. We can all get to know our human rights and talk about why we should never take them for granted. People are more likely to listen to friends or family than experts and are more willing to take action when it's important to someone they know. We can all try to respect each other, help each other and protect those in need.

HUMAN RIGHTS TIMELINE

Here is a list of some of the moments in history covered in this book that help to tell the story of the fight for human rights.

c. 1200 – 323 BCE: The ancient Greeks are the first people known to have talked about human rights.

CE 1215: King John of England signs the Magna Carta. This historic document stated that everyone – including the king – had to obey laws. He didn't actually want to sign it, but did so to try to stop his barons turning against him and starting a civil war. Civil war did break out and the Magna Carta failed, but it has helped to inspire and define the rights and laws that we have today.

1774–92: King Louis XVI reigns France.

1775: The first battles of the American Revolution take place in the state of Massachusetts.

1776: US Congress votes for independence on 2 July; the United States Declaration of Independence was adopted on 4 July and formally signed on 2 August.

1789–99: The French Revolution is a period of unrest and change in France. It becomes a republic with a government deciding laws and the ex-king (Louis XVI) is executed in 1793.

1914–18: The First World War kills millions and forces millions more people from their homes.

1939–45: The Second World War causes the deaths and displacement of millions of people.

1948: The Universal Declaration of Human Rights is created and is adopted by 48 countries around the world. The first Human Rights Day is held.

1959: The UN creates the Declaration of the Rights of the Child to give children extra protections.

1961: Amnesty International is founded by English barrister, Peter Benenson.

1964: Almost 200 years after the signing of the US Declaration of Independence, the 1964 Civil Rights Act finally gives all US citizens the right to vote.

1989: The Tiananmen Square uprising occurs in Beijing, China. Thousands of students and activists call for (among other things) democracy and freedom of speech. Hundreds are killed when Chinese troops open fire.

1989: A human rights treaty called The United Nations Convention on the Rights of the Child is created. As of 2021 the rights in it are law in 196 countries of the world.

2008: Pakistani schoolgirl, Malala Yousafzai, is shot to try to stop her speaking out about education for girls. She becomes famous worldwide and continues to campaign for girls' rights.

2014: Malala Yousafzai wins the Nobel Peace Prize.

2017: Divina Maloum wins the International Children's Peace Prize for her work with children exposed to violence.

2018: Swedish environmental activist, Greta Thunberg, holds her first 'School Strike for Climate' protest.

GLOSSARY

activist someone who campaigns to bring about political or social change

ancient Greece a civilisation that flourished from c. 1200 BCE to 323 BCE in what is now Greece and the lands around the Mediterranean Sea

atmosphere the layer of gases that surround Earth

charter a set of rules or promises that everyone has to obey

climate the usual weather in an area or country

climate change the warming of Earth as a result of the gas, carbon dioxide, being produced by burning fossil fuels

declaration a formal statement; in this case a document that says that the US will rule itself and not be governed by the British Crown

environment the natural world

fossil fuel natural fuels, such as coal and gas, that formed millions of years ago from the remains of living plants and animals.

French Revolution the events that overthrew the political system and society in France, and which took place from 1789–99

government a group of people who rule a country

illegal against the law

independence to be independent is to be free from outside control or authority

lead a type of soft, heavy metal

marine relating to or found in the sea

overthrow to remove from power

pollution substances that can harm or poison the environment, people or animals

restrict to put a limit on or keep under control

sanitation referring to clean water and safe sewage disposal

solar relating to the Sun

solemn formal; serious

terrorism violence – often against ordinary people – that usually has a political aim

torture when severe pain is used as a punishment or to force someone to do or say something

BOOKS TO READ

Children in Our World: Rights and Equality
by Marie Murray and illustrated by Hanane Kai (Wayland, 2021)

I'm a Global Citizen: Human Rights
by Alice Harman and illustrated by David Broadbent (Franklin Watts, 2020)

I'm a Global Citizen: Rules for Everyone
by Georgia Amson-Bradshaw and illustrated by David Broadbent (Franklin Watts, 2020)

Malala
by Malala Yousafzai (Wren and Rook, 2018)

INDEX

America 8, 30
Amnesty International 13, 30
Anti-Slavery International 25

Beijing 17, 30
Benenson, Peter 30
Black people 9

Cameroon 23
children's rights 14-15
China 17, 30
Civil Rights Act (USA) 30
climate change 26-27, 30, 31
Colorado, USA 21

Declaration of Independence 8, 30, 31
Declaration of the Rights of the Child 15, 30

First World War 10, 30
forced marriage 12-13
fossil fuels 26, 31
freedom of speech 16-17
French Revolution 9, 30, 31

Greece/Greeks, ancient 6, 30, 31

human rights (definition) 4
Human Rights Day 28, 30
human trafficking 25

International Children's Peace Prize 23, 30

King John 7, 30
King Louis XVI 9, 30, 31

Liu Xiaobo 17

Magna Carta (Great Charter) 7
Maloum, Divina 23, 30
Native Americans 9
natural law 6
New York, USA 27
Nobel Peace Prize 17, 19, 30

pollution 21, 31

Rao, Gitanjali 21
revolution 8-9, 30, 31
Roosevelt, Eleanor 11

Roosevelt, Franklin D. 11

school/schooling 18-19
Second World War 10, 30
slavery 24-25

Tethys, Greek goddess 21
Thunberg, Greta 27, 30
Tiananmen Square protests (1989) 17, 30

UN Convention on the Rights of the Child 15, 30
United Nations 10, 28
Universal Declaration of Human Rights 11, 30

violence 22-23

water and sanitation 20-21, 31
women's rights 9, 12-13

Yousafzai, Malala 19, 30

Franklin Watts
First published in Great Britain in 2021 by The Watts Publishing Group
Copyright © The Watts Publishing Group, 2021

All rights reserved.

HB ISBN: 978 1 4451 7145 6
PB ISBN: 978 1 4451 7146 3

Printed and bound in Dubai

Editor: Amy Pimperton
Designer: Peter Scoulding
Cover design: Peter Scoulding
Illustrations: Toby Newsome

Page 2 photograph
© Professor Leslie Thomas QC

FSC
www.fsc.org
MIX
Paper | Supporting responsible forestry
FSC® C104740

Franklin Watts, an imprint of
Hachette Children's Group
Carmelite House
50 Victoria Embankment
London EC4Y 0DZ

An Hachette UK Company
www.hachette.co.uk
www.franklinwatts.co.uk

All facts and statistics were correct at the time of printing.

The authorised representative in the EEA is Hachette Ireland, 8 Castlecourt Centre, Dublin 15, D15 XTP3, Ireland (email: info@hbgi.ie)